# SCIENCE
# AND THE
# QUEST
# FOR
# MEANING

by Donald M. MacKay

Introduction by John North

*Grand Rapids*
WILLIAM B. EERDMANS PUBLISHING COMPANY

Copyright © 1982
by Wm. B. Eerdmans Publishing Company
255 Jefferson Ave. S.E., Grand Rapids, Mich. 49503
All rights reserved
Printed in the United States of America

*Based on the author's Pascal lecture
series given in 1979 at the
University of Waterloo, Ontario.*

**Library of Congress Cataloging in Publication Data**

MacKay, Donald MacCrimmon, 1922-
    *Science and the quest for meaning.*

1. Religion and science—1946-    —Addresses,
    essays, lectures. I. Title.
    BL241:M18      261.5'5      81-17504
    ISBN 0-8028-1914-1      AACR2

# Contents

v

# Introduction

Here is the second in the series of Pascal Lectures on Christianity and the University at the University of Waterloo, delivered by Professor MacKay in October 1979. Blaise Pascal (1623-1662), the seventeenth-century French academic and Christian, is remembered today as a forerunner of Newton in the establishment of infinitesimal calculus, and as the author of the Christian meditations *Les Pensées*. Members of the University of Waterloo, wishing to establish a forum for presenting Christian issues in an academic environment, have chosen to commemorate Pascal's spirit with the annual lecture series bearing his name.

The Pascal Lectures bring to the University of Waterloo outstanding individuals of international repute who have distinguished themselves in both an area of scholarly endeavor and an area of Christian thought or life. These individuals converse with the university community about an aspect of its world—its theories, its research, its leadership role in our society—challenging the university to search for truth through personal faith and intellectual inquiry.

For the past thirty years Donald MacKay has been

one of the world's foremost thinkers on the organization of the brain. His wartime work on radar with the British Admiralty led him to develop the theory of communication, computing, and control which he has applied since 1951 to the elucidation of brain mechanisms, especially those of vision and hearing. He is also well known to philosophers as a writer who explores the relationship between brain and mind. He has held distinguished lectureships at universities in Britain (Oxford, Cambridge, London, Stirling, Newcastle) and in the United States (Johns Hopkins and the University of California, Berkeley). His contributions to scholarly scientific organizations have included joint editorship of the journal *Experimental Brain Research* and of the international *Handbook of Sensory Physiology*, membership in the Council of the International Brain Research Organization, and chairmanship of the Commission on Communication and Control Processes of the International Union of Pure and Applied Biophysics. In 1960 Dr. MacKay founded Keele University's Research Department of Communication and Neuroscience, where he has remained as professor and head of the department.

The books that Professor MacKay has written and edited provide a Christian perspective for students of science who seek an integrated world view, and make it clear that he shares Pascal's convictions about both the importance and the limitations of the mind:

> Let us then strive to think well; that is the basic principle of morality.
>
> *Pensée 200*

> It is the heart which perceives God and not the reason. That is what faith is: God perceived by the heart, not by the reason.
>
> *Pensée 424*

Like Pascal, too, he believes in the wholeness of our universe as presented by biblical Christian theism; and, as he explains in *The Clockwork Image* (1973), he also believes that an essential, non-accidental harmony exists between the Christian doctrine of the natural world and the spirit and practice of natural science. Thus biblical faith, far from being in conflict with the study of science, has liberating implications for scientific pursuits and for all properly critical thinking. In particular, as MacKay argues in *Brains, Machines and Persons* (1980), the science of the brain does not threaten orthodox Christian faith, does not distance us from the Christian view of man, but is thoroughly and harmoniously complementary to it. Pascal says it well:

> Those people do honour to nature who tell her that she can talk of anything, even theology.
>
> *Pensée 675*

A notable trend in contemporary higher education, research, and scholarship is the growing separation of scientific and humanistic studies. Very seldom now is a baccalaureate degree, that standard measure of a university education, presented jointly by the disciplines of art and science (though Professor MacKay's own University of Keele is in this respect an honorable exception). One of the consequences throughout the Western world is a fragmented perspective of man and his world. Thus the scientist and the humanist are developing increasingly hardened attitudes toward each other, each expressing growing confidence in the significance and authority of his own field, and at least implying the sufficiency of that field, with its assumptions and methodology, as a self-contained area of study. Each may even act as if the study of that narrow field vindicated his existence.

In these two lectures on the meaning of science, Donald MacKay the scientist restores a broader view, defending the pursuit of science against those who fear that contemporary scientific studies trample our dignity and deny our imagination in the name of rationalism. Moreover, he does so on religious as well as humanistic grounds. He argues that although science and technology do not themselves answer the ultimate questions of meaning, they are to be welcomed as an immense enrichment of human life; they should steadily build our confidence in precedent ("scientific laws") as a guide to our expectations in the natural world, and therefore should enrich our praise of the Creator for his trustworthiness. The consequence of this increased scientific knowledge is a responsibility to practically apply it to improve the human condition. This, too, is an echo of Pascal:

> We make an idol of truth itself, for truth apart from charity is not God, but his image and an idol that we must not love or worship. Still less must we love or worship its opposite, which is falsehood.
>
> *Pensée 926*

Few readers of this volume will have had the privilege of meeting Donald MacKay. I have dined with his family in their home on the outskirts of Keele, joining him, his wife Valerie, and their five children as they considered the Scriptures and prayed for each other at the end of a busy day. I have also watched him, under the stress of travel, lecture in an unfamiliar environment to a large, unfamiliar group, and maintain an attitude both gentle and tenacious in the discussions, however ill-informed or ill-mannered the questioner. These two experiences provided the comforting reassurance that this intellectual is a person of warmth, strength, consistency, and wholeness.

JOHN S. NORTH
*University of Waterloo*

# Does Science
# Destroy Meaning?

THE primary question I wish to address in these lectures is this: CAN SCIENCE PROVIDE AN ANSWER TO THE QUEST FOR MEANING?

There was a time not so many years ago when many of the popular prophets would have said "Yes" to this question. Scientists who would have called themselves atheists or agnostics preached the gospel of what they called "scientific humanism." By applying the principles of science some of them even thought they could develop ethical systems to guide human conduct. Now, as will become clear, I think they were mistaken. But in our day, I believe the pendulum has swung to the other extreme, and with a violence which I fear is equally misguided. Loud voices are now being raised to condemn the scientist as the arch destroyer of meaning, the spoiler-in-chief of our community.

This is not altogether a new phenomenon. Many of you who are more literate than I may remember Keats's lines in "Lamia":

> Do not all charms fly
> At the mere touch of cold philosophy?

There was an awful rainbow once in heaven:
We know her woof, her texture; she is given
In the dull catalogue of common things.

(11. 229-33)

Or you may think of Charles Dickens' biting satire of certain scientific attitudes in the novel *Hard Times*. You may remember how Chapter One begins, with the ranting of Thomas Gradgrind, the governor of the school:

> "Now, what I want is Facts. Teach these boys and girls nothing but Facts. Facts alone are wanted in life. Plant nothing else, and root out everything else. You can only form the minds of reasoning animals upon Facts; nothing else will ever be of any service to them. . . . Stick to Facts, sir!"

Dickens then sums up Gradgrind in a caustic description:

> The speaker and the schoolmaster and the third grown person present all backed a little, and swept with their eyes the inclined plane of little vessels then and there arranged in order ready to have imperial gallons of facts poured into them until they were full to the brim.
>
> THOMAS GRADGRIND, sir. A man of realities. A man of facts and calculations. A man who proceeds upon the principle that two and two are four, and nothing over, and who is not to be talked into allowing for anything over. Thomas Gradgrind, sir—peremptorily Thomas—Thomas Gradgrind. With a rule and a pair of scales, and the multiplication table always in his pocket, sir, ready to weigh and measure any parcel of human nature, and tell you exactly

what it comes to. It is a mere question of figures, a case of simple arithmetic.

Thus Dickens. And in our own time, of course, we have such phenomena as Theodore Roszak, to whom scientific expertise is

A bewilderingly perverse effort to demonstrate that nothing, *absolutely nothing*, is particularly special, unique or marvellous, but can be lowered to the status of mechanized routine. More and more the spirit of 'nothing but' hovers over advanced scientific research: the effort to degrade, disenchant, level down. Is it that the creative and the joyous embarrass the scientific mind to such an extent that it must try with might and main to degrade them?[1]

Again, the feeling is the same: the scientist is the destroyer of meaning. Here Roszak rather echoes Nietzsche, who you may remember saw the whole history of science since Copernicus as "an unbroken progress in the self-belittling of man. All science nowadays," he complained, "sets out to talk man out of his present opinion of himself."

These are only a few samples of the negative reaction to science. And today, for good or ill, the cult of science-bashing has plenty of devotees. According to them, the way to recover our lost sense of meaning is to turn our backs on scientifically disciplined habits of thought and drop out of the technological society.

Now you might perhaps expect me as a Christian to

[1]Theodore Roszak, *The Making of a Counter Culture* (New York: Anchor, 1969; rpt. London: Faber, 1970), p. 229.

have at least a fellow-traveler's sympathy for this line of protest. But I must confess that I have nothing of the kind. What I want to argue here is that, from a thoroughgoing Christian perspective, science and technology are in principle to be positively welcomed as an immense enrichment of the meaningfulness of human life, even if they do not of themselves answer the ultimate questions of meaning. Indeed, a consistent Christian believer has a stronger incentive than anyone else to make what contribution he can to scientific and technological advancement, provided that this is carried on in the spirit of responsible stewardship that is taught in the Bible.

## CRITICISMS OF THE SCIENTIFIC APPROACH

But first let us see what is true in the highly emotive case argued by the anti-scientist. I have a number of headings here, and I think that what we should perhaps do is pick up under each heading a feature of the scientific approach, see why it causes offense to these sensitive defenders of the human spirit, and then see how we ourselves should react to the threat that they point out.

First—and this is the sort of thing, I think, that particularly offends people like Roszak—science does adopt and insist on strict criteria for what counts as valid scientific evidence and valid inference. For the scientist, mere opinion is not enough, and even mere demonstration of logical coherence is not enough. He has to go further and show that if what he is claiming were not the case, then some facts of experience would not be as indeed they are. This emphasis on fact, then, is very down-to-earth and understandably threatening to someone whose life revolves around the world of the imagination. And it *is* possible to teach science in such a way as to devalue the role of the human imagination and to desiccate the aspiring scientist before he ever gets into the practice of science. But we have only to read the writings of the leading scientists, those who have made great discoveries, to recognize that the practice of science at its best is a cooperative exercise in which imagination plays just as vital a part as respect for facts.

What the scientist does is expose his whole being, particularly his imagination, to the challenge of what he has tried in every way to identify as solid facts. He presents himself with these facts, knowing that there will be no routine way of grinding out valid conclusions from them. His aim, rather, is to have his imagination stimulated so that, with luck, he might hit on a hypothesis worth testing, one that might account for what produces the facts that intrigue him. And any good science teacher will treasure any gifts that his pupils have for imagination just as much as he will treasure their ability to reason logically. The teaching of science is above all a human enterprise. It is the passing on, not merely of facts or technique, but of a craft, an attitude, a spirit in which the interaction of the scientist with his data can spur the imagination on to make new discoveries about the principles on which the natural world is organized. The hallmark here, I suggest, is obedience.

Now this is a long way from the image of the scientist

as essentially a dominating manipulator of nature. But what the early founders of modern science had to discover—and they were stimulated to do this, as you will find if you read Bacon, by their reading of the Bible—is that anyone who wants to have dominion over nature must begin by listening, observing, respecting, and obeying the implications of the facts; by not bringing preconceived ideas, as the medieval predecessors of modern science did, to the natural world and insisting that nature should dance, as it were, to their tune composed beforehand. Such a person must be ready to have his imagination disciplined by the data.

### Rationality vs. Rationalism

This brings out a vital distinction which is often neglected in the anti-scientific propaganda of our day: the distinction between rationality, which is an attempt to be obedient with one's mind to the implications of the data one has, and rationalism, which is an attitude that sits in judgment on what ought to be, on the grounds that my predilections make **this** attractive to my reason and **that** not.

Now, I'm not denying that there are stages, perhaps particularly in a subject like theoretical physics, when purely aesthetic considerations have guided scientists; they have discovered principles (as they tell you in their autobiographies) simply by playing a hunch that was attractive to them. What I am suggesting, though, is that if a scientist goes through his daily life, in effect putting nature on the Procrustean bed of his own preferences and ignoring whatever does not fit in with his predilections, then he is moving in the opposite direction of healthy science. And this rationalistic attitude, which says, "I can't believe that electrons would be composed of such-and-such," this authoritarian attitude which has occasionally cropped up in the history of science, is always a barrier.

When we read attacks on science, then, based on the grounds that it is rationalistic, I think we have to bear this distinction particularly in mind. Science indeed ought to be rational, as any honest man ought, in order to follow out the implications of what he knows or believes to be fact. But rationality is not the same as rationalism. I'm going to argue, in fact, that in this strictness about what follows from what, and what counts as valid criteria of evidence and so forth, the scientist is far from being an enemy to meaningfulness generally; in fact, he is expressing the most open attitude possible for the discovery of meaning, an attitude that is essentially, though not exclusively, Christian.

### The Spectator Standpoint

Now, secondly, science is much berated because it adopts and recommends what we might call a spectator's standpoint. The scientist tries to describe the world as it would be even if he weren't there. At least that is classically the scientific effort, the emphasis being on withdrawal and detachment from the situation described. And you'll find many people condemning even this approach on the grounds that it's unnatural to partition the world into "that out there" and "me here" when, if we think about it, all of our experience is participation between us and our environment. These critics accuse science of distorting reality.

But if we think about it, we realize that the scientist doesn't adopt the spectator's standpoint because he wants, as it were, a particularly distorted but convenient version of reality to play with. He adopts it for essentially communal purposes. The scientist sees himself as the "mapmaker" of his community, and he has other mapmakers to cooperate with. It is vital that the mapmakers be able to compare data, and therefore it is vital that they be able to express their picture of the world from a standpoint that is shareable by others—a spectator's standpoint in the sense that one scientist can bow out and another take his place. So to attack the scientist on the grounds that he praises detachment, as if this meant the same thing as adopting a lofty and disdainful attitude toward the real world, is totally to misrepresent and misunderstand what science is all about.

Having said that, though, let me again say that science badly taught—and I wish I could believe that it weren't often badly taught—can inculcate this kind of lofty disdain for the muddy untidiness of the real world. The scientist can become a kind of intellectual snob who won't bother with a problem that can't be parceled up neatly and observed for the sake of prediction. So that it's not altogether wide of the mark to warn scientists against this as a danger; and indeed it can take the form of a sort of paralysis of commitment, a paralysis of the natural human capacity for committing oneself when the data are rather scanty. Professionally, of course, the scientist is prohibited from publishing a finding unless the data are strong enough to make the odds, let us say, more than twenty-to-one against the possibility that he's been deceived by chance. That's just a standard routine for keeping a lot of shabby claims from cluttering up the literature that future generations have to read. And in that sense, commitment on the basis of inadequate evidence is professional suicide. A scientist must try to make statements about the physical world that are reliable enough for his fellow mapmakers to build on.

But this attitude toward publishable data, this reluctance to commit oneself on the basis of inadequate evidence, need not and must not be allowed to extend to the affairs of everyday life. A scientist, if he sows seed in his garden, doesn't refuse to do so unless he is guaranteed that nineteen out of twenty of the seeds will germinate, or anything of that sort. Scientists are capable of preserving their attitude of caution and their reluctance to commit themselves in their professional lives without losing the common touch. True, if science is badly taught, then the generation listening to the badly taught scientists can get the wrong idea. They may think that exercising this caution is a fine way to prevent themselves from being let down by life, and end up being the sort who are never taken in, never able to commit themselves unless they've got good solid guarantees.

On this point J. H. Oldham makes a significant

remark in a little book called *Life is Commitment*, which is very well worth reading. "To refuse to choose," he says, "is to choose to drift. It is a refusal of responsibility and consequently of life in its full human meaning." And Oldham is right: if this attitude of cautious detachment is allowed to overtake the whole of the scientist's life, then to some extent he loses his life, loses some of its full human meaning. But again, this is a totally unnecessary consequence of being a good scientist.

### The "Impersonal"

A third criticism of science is that it has changed our vague, woolly, and perhaps superstitious attitude toward natural events into a belief that nature is a theatre of purely impersonal forces. Science in its modern form began with a strong emphasis on what has been called the "de-deification" of nature. The Greek tradition saw nature as quasi-divine, almost a living being. It was sensible to attribute to nature purposes, desires, tendencies, and so on. The mechanistic science that became popular at the time of the founding of the Royal Society took the deity out of nature; it insisted, on biblical grounds (e.g., Genesis 1), that nature was a created entity, like man himself, but a non-divine entity, given to us by God for responsible development.

Science had a biblical emphasis, then, the sort of thing which I would suggest Christians have nothing to be ashamed of. But there have been critics (and they have a point—Toynbee is one example) who have taken offense at the removal of the divine element from nature. Toynbee would say that man, having de-deified nature, has felt free to rape the natural world, to dominate it in a selfish manner, behavior that is now causing his own destruction.[2] I myself think that Toynbee exaggerates, and perhaps he meant to provoke us. But it is a fair point that if we lose the attitude of stewardship which the Bible also inculcates, if we forget that our biblical notion of dominion over nature includes the responsibility of answering to a Creator who has given us that dominion, then very easily our com-

---

[2]The following excerpts from an article by Toynbee in *Horizon*, XV (1973), 6-9, indicate the spirit in which he writes: "According to the Bible, God had created the world; the world was his to do what he liked with; he had chosen to license Adam and Eve to do what *they* liked with it; and their license was not canceled by the Fall. Genesis I, 28, gave the license; Genesis III, 19, provided the incentive. The thesis of this essay, then, is that some of the major maladies of the present-day world—in particular the recklessly extravagant consumption of nature's irreplaceable treasures, and the pollution of those of them that man has not already devoured—can be traced back to a religious cause, and that this cause is the rise of monotheism. . . . Monotheism, as enunciated in the Book of Genesis, has removed the age-old restraint that was once placed on man's greed by his awe.

"The directive given in the first chapter of the Book of Genesis . . . has turned out to be bad advice, and we are beginning, wisely, to recoil from it."

As an essay in scholarly exposition, this is deplorable. Man's license in biblical terms is that of a *steward* of God's gifts, not a selfish exploiter. The Pentateuch itself issues stringent commands against feckless mismanagement of natural resources. Toynbee's declared hatred of monotheism seems here to have gotten the better of his academic conscience.

mand over a secularized nature can become something self-centered and, in the end, self-destructive.

The other accusation, by Keats, that the de-deification of nature destroys wonder, is a little more difficult to defend. It is perfectly true that when we understand the colors of the rainbow as a scientist would explain them, in terms of the refraction of light, then at a certain level we say, "Now I see how the trick is done," and we may even discover how to do the same sort of trick ourselves with a garden hose and a spotlight. So that kind of wonder, about how it is done, is removed at a certain level. But any scientist will tell you that the more he discovers about the field in which he is doing research, the more, when he thinks about it, it strikes him with awe. The sheer marvel of the complexity of the interacting pattern of activity that he studies leads any scientist worth his salt to an attitude close to worship, whether he's religious or not. You can look at the writings of any of the great scientists and find this kind of awe expressed. In principle at least, then, it is simply false to say that the de-deification of nature automatically brings with it any reduction of the wonder which the scientist feels on contemplating the natural world.

### Chance

Now I want to move to another level of science, for which, it has to be admitted, some scientists have done what might be called a bad public relations job. I am talking about the field of chance, which, incidentally, was a field to which Pascal made one of the first theoretical contributions. He was one of those who worked out some of the simpler mathematics of probability, for the benefit, I believe, of some of his friends interested in gambling.

In science today chance is not only an index of our ignorance. True, the chance of drawing a black ball out of a bag full of black and white balls is something we calculate on the assumption that *we don't know* where the balls are in the bag, rather than as indicating that the actual behavior of the balls is indeterminate. But chance in physics has in this century come to bear a deeper significance. It has been found experimentally that when subatomic particles such as electrons interact, or are blown apart in the disintegration of an atom, then the way they rebound is not determined exactly by any of the laws known to physics. Instead, there is a fuzz of uncertainty about the predicted paths of the particles. By speaking of an element of "chance" in such encounters, then, the physicist means not only that we *don't* know exactly how they will work out, but that we *can't* know. The equations we use in physics, the theoretical models we use, and the methods we use to get our data are such that when one gets down to the level of microparticles, there isn't in the whole of physics an equation that fully determines the behavior of any of those particles.

There have been those who have argued from this fact that our world must be looked at as a much less meaningful place than we originally thought it was. One of the most notable of these is the biologist Jacques

Monod, who in 1971 published *Chance and Necessity*, a book essentially about the role of chance in biology. In it, he says:

> Chance alone is at the source of every innovation, of all creation in the biosphere: pure chance, absolutely free but blind, at the very root of the stupendous edifice of evolution. This central concept of biology is today the sole conceivable hypothesis, the only one compatible with observed and tested facts. The biosphere looks like the product of a unique event whose chances of occurring were almost nil. The universe was not pregnant with life. Our number came up in the Monte Carlo game.

And on these grounds Monod claims that "man at last knows that he is alone in the unfeeling immensity of the universe out of which he emerged only by chance." He claims further that these discoveries make it impossible to believe in any concept of a Creator.

Now, any anti-scientist who wants ammunition and who has some sympathy for a religious view of life doesn't need much more than this sort of utterance to justify his vigor. But I contend that, for all Monod's eminence as a scientist, he is here perpetrating a philosophical blunder, confusing two fundamentally different notions of chance. Chance as a scientific concept is essentially an indicator of our uncertainty about what is likely to follow from given circumstances. We speak about the chance of drawing out the black ball from the bag, because we are uncertain where the balls are lying in the bag. We speak about the chances of an electron rebounding in a given direction, not only because we don't know where it is, but because even if we did know, the laws of physics wouldn't allow us to predict with any precision in what direction it would rebound. But in either case, chance is not a name for an entity "out there" that does things. It is simply a name for our own ignorance of what's going to happen. It is a quantitative measure, but it is not in any sense an entity, so it makes no sense to credit it with initiative in the way that Monod does when he talks about it as "absolutely free but blind," and so forth.

The other notion of chance, with which Monod confuses the scientific notion, is a pagan mythological concept: Chance (with a capital C) as a kind of deity—the deity of chaos. Though he professes to speak as a scientist, what Monod says makes sense only as a reference to some kind of capricious agent—an alternative to the God of order. Talk about such a crazy deity is indeed a rival alternative to Christian talk of a rational and coherent Creator. But what is quite clear, once you look at it, is that nothing in Monod's *science* justifies this way of talking. So it is not his science, but his metaphysics, which lies at the back of his atheistic interpretation of the theory of the random origin of living molecules from which he starts.

If you go back to the biblical view of the natural world, just, as it were, looking at the alternative view to see what would follow from it, then nothing is clearer in the biblical theology of nature than that the Bible regards all events in our world—whether or not they are random or "chance" in a scientific sense—as attributable to the agency of God. Even when people draw lots (according to the book of Proverbs), "the whole disposing thereof is of the Lord." In other words, the Creator of whom the Bible speaks is one who gives being to the whole space-time in which we find ourselves, every event in it—just as, to use Dorothy Sayers' analogy, a novelist has to give being to all the events that occur in her novel, whether or not some of these are chance occurrences in the world of the participants.

Thus it is a mistake to suggest that, from the standpoint of biblical theism, a theory of the origin of biological molecules that traces the chain of events back to one labeled "random" or "chance" is an exclusive *alternative* to the biblical doctrine of the origin of all things in God as Creator. The truth is the opposite. Monod's *scientific* hypothesis, for what it is worth, fits as peaceably in the biblical view of things as any other, because the only question at issue is the factual one of what kind of a story our Creator has in fact written. Chance in its scientific sense, then, is not the name of an agent; and therefore any suggestion that the scientist's admission of chance is anti-theistic is based on confusion.

## The Second Law of Thermodynamics

Now, there is another closely related feature of science which has been much-discussed and has, in fact, even found its way into the popular songs of Flanders and Swann. In their album *At the Drop of Another Hat* (one of the best hour's worth of laughs I know), they actually sing a song about the first and second laws of thermodynamics. The first law simply states that work and heat are equivalent. The essence of the second law is that in any process in which heat is exchanged, the orderliness of the energy that is exchanged decreases. Or, to put it the other way around, energy tends to get scrambled in the process of exchange. If this law is applied to all events in the universe, it suggests that all the exchanges of energy in the universe must, over the course of millennia, lead to the gradual smearing out of energy, so that eventually all the interesting things that go on around us now will cease to happen, because everything will have come to much the same temperature and nothing more will be left to occur. That is the notion, at any rate, which many people have extrapolated from the second law of thermodynamics. Some people have concluded that this law implies that our universe is bound to end in chaos, the so-called "heat death of the universe." Once again, it is a strike against the scientist: he is ruining our hopes for the future by producing a law which predicts that in the end everything is going to run down, or, as Flanders and Swann put it, "It's going to cool down and there'll be no more work, and there'll be perfect peace."

Now, here again it seems to me we have a confusion. In the first place, the second law of thermodynamics is framed for what is called a closed system. In other words, if one is being strict about it, it says only that within any system that is *totally enclosed* so that all its exchanges are kept within boundaries, the chaos will increase on an average within those boundaries. That's fair enough; but when we try to apply this law to the whole universe, the question that is unresolved is whether the universe can be properly described for scientific purposes as a closed system. So this is the first point: science does not, in fact, unambiguously justify this kind of conclusion about our whole universe.

But the second point as far as theology is concerned is this: nowhere in the Christian gospel is there a suggestion that our world is bound to go on and on into infinity, becoming a better and better place. Quite the contrary. The Christian hope is that our Creator, having worked those purposes for which He has brought our world into being, will write a new story in which those who have come to know and love Him here will find themselves. But it will be a new story, not a mere extrapolation of the old one into some infinite future. I suggest that those who regard the second law of thermodynamics as a threat to the meaningfulness of what the Christian believes about life are mistaking, on the one hand, the technical competence of the second law to predict a chaotic end for the universe, and, on the other, the nature of the Christian hope.

### Reductionism

But now we come to an idea that is more general and in some ways more difficult to cope with because it comes up in so many different forms. It is what is often called "reductionism," or, as I like to call it, "nothing-but-ery." It is typified by saying, "Once you look into it scientifically, what you think is A is nothing but B." And if the scientist has done his sums correctly he can usually justify the second part of the statement, which has a demoralizing effect on the layman particularly: he feels that he is being robbed.

There are a good many popular writers of science who, I'm afraid, lend credence to this. Take, for example, Desmond Morris's book, *The Naked Ape*. His thesis is that man can be regarded for scientific purposes as nothing more than, nothing but, one of the apes. The jacket of Morris's book says, "Since he first became intellectually aware, man has indulged in lofty and exhaustive inquiries into his own nature. Now this ethological analysis by an eminent zoologist puts him firmly in his place alongside the 192 other species of apes and monkeys, among which man is most easily distinguished by the nakedness of his skin." So you see that there is some justification for the complaint of those who say that science is out to destroy the human image. Or take Richard Dawkins' book, *The Selfish Gene*, which has a great many ingenious and entertaining things to say. But the jacket copy again declares that "Richard Dawkins introduces us to ourselves as we really are" (note the word "really"), telling us we are "throwaway survival machines for our immortal genes. Man is a gene machine, blindly programmed to preserve its selfish genes."

It is hardly surprising if those who value human nature react to such claims by saying, "If this is science I don't want it, it's nasty." And it's very easy to be tempted to respond in a manner that virtually gives away the game to these clever blurb writers. Because if you take away the question-begging words "merely" and "really" and ask what it is that is being said as a matter of scientific fact, then in each case I suggest that the facts are neutral and not in the least damaging to human dignity. Take a human pelt and put it alongside other pelts of other species and you will identify the human one by its nakedness. So what? That's what you would expect. Man from that standpoint belongs to the classification of the apes, and the fact that he is naked is just the easy way of identifying which skin is his.

Similarly, it may well be true—a very ingenious point by Dawkins—that from a certain genetic point of view the entity which is preserved through reproduction is the genetic specification, rather than the species, or whatever. If you fasten on the genetic specification and say, "That's the thing that's really out to preserve itself," then you can make very interesting and illuminating new appraisals of the process that you're studying. But again, this is a neutral fact. Why shouldn't it be so?

The fallacy in both of these cases, I suggest, is the fallacy of reductionism or "nothing-but-ery," which is suggesting that once you have a complete story at one level, or claim you have a complete story, you leave no room for any other story of the meaning or significance of the situation at another level. And I suggest that it's important not to respond to this kind of "nothing-but-ery" by attacking the science. If we do spot a flaw in the scientific argument, then as an act of charity to a fellow scientist we ought to get on with pointing it out. But to hunt for flaws in the scientific description in the hope of rescuing the significance of the other level would be to give the game away completely. The key to this sort of situation is to recognize that completeness of description at one level doesn't necessarily rule out the need for descriptions at others.

Think of looking through a microscope at a newspaper page at varying degrees of magnification. When you examine it very closely, you can't see much more than a lot of inky blobs. If you reduce the magnification, though, pulling back a little from what is being presented, you see now what you might believe to be a part of a letter of the alphabet. What you discover eventually is that it is a letter *e*. Here we have a situation in which the initial description, in terms of ink blobs, could have been complete, but it would have missed the point that what we have here is a letter *e*. Describing this as "a letter *e* and nothing but a letter *e*" would be just as accurate as describing it as "ink blobs on paper, and nothing but ink blobs on paper." It's a question of choice of level, and the completeness of the one description doesn't in the least prove that you don't need the other or that it isn't valid.

Now imagine what might happen if you reduced magnification still further, steadily increasing your viewing distance. You find that what you've been looking at is the *e* in the middle of the word "independence," and that that word in turn is in the middle of an inflammatory article about politics; here is a whole new level of significance, not at all a *rival* of the others, but systematically ignored by them.

Nor can the higher level of meaning be down-graded as a mere "optional extra," as if the lower-level account was somehow more "realistic." The motorist who drives past a "NO ENTRY" sign, dismissing it as nothing but enamel on metal, may be scientifically accurate; but the arm of the law could soon disabuse him of the idea that this was the most "realistic" view of the sign!

So you see the point is a very simple one. It is false to suggest that if you can completely describe man as nothing but a mass of molecules, or nothing but a population of nerve cells acting according to physical laws, or nothing but a carrier of selfish genes, then you have invalidated other levels of significance in man. It is a philosophical blunder of the worst sort, a disgrace to science; and one has at this point some sympathy with people who are taken in by these claims and as a result attack science. But it is not science that should be the target: science doesn't of itself deserve any of the blame that falls deservedly on the heads of those who try to degrade human dignity in the name of these descriptions.

## The Bogey of Determinism

We've been skirting round—or leading up to—what many people see as the biggest threat of science to the meaningfulness of life: determinism. Determinism, as I've already mentioned, is not part of the apparatus of theoretical physics anymore. The theoretical physicist calculates probabilities, and has given up the hope of using his present system to calculate outcomes absolutely, precisely, in a determinate way. But I think we would be very mistaken to imagine that this affects in principle the deterministic character of science itself. It would be just tomfoolery, for example, for me to pretend that the result of flipping a light switch isn't, for all practical purposes, "physically determined." In this sense science still, by and large, works with the concept of determination.

This is true particularly in human science, an area in which we might feel—and I think the enemies of science do feel—that determinism is least welcome. We might feel that we'd like the scientist to keep his detached and predictive hands off our bodies. But of course when we put ourselves in the hands of the doctor for medical treatment, our attitude suddenly changes, and we long for him to know more of what determines what, in order that he can do his best to ensure that we will be healthy. What I'm suggesting is that, if you look into it, it is false to claim that determinism at a physical level destroys human dignity; this accusation exhibits the same kind of fallacy as the idea that scientific descriptions of man damage his dignity. We all know the story of the little girl who said to the judge, "It ain't my fault, judge, it's my glands." And Dickens' story of Gradgrind illustrates the same philosophical principle through an interesting twist—Gradgrind's son commits a crime, and is found out:

> "If a thunderbolt had fallen on me," said the father, "it would have shocked me less than this."

"I don't see why," grumbled the son. "So many people are employed in situations of trust. So many people out of so many will be dishonest. I've heard you talk of it a hundred times, its being a law. How can I help laws? You've comforted others with such things, father, comfort yourself."

This notion—that physical determinism relieves individuals of responsibility for their actions—has quite an ancient pedigree. Indeed, it can be traced back to the Greeks. But is it in fact rational? Does it follow that if you had a completely determinate physical story about the goings-on in a man's brain when he decided to do something, then the outcome would not be determined by his choosing? I suggest that it would be quite fallacious to infer this; that we've got to recognize that determination at one level doesn't exclude determination at another. Now you may say this sounds very abstruse, an example of begging the question, but as a matter of fact there is today a very common illustration which we all accept—the way in which people use computers. Not all of us use them, but we all suffer the consequences of their being used on our electricity bills and our income-tax accounts.

If you were to ask the tax man who has produced your bill just what has determined the behavior of the computer, he would take great pains to show you that its calculations were determined by certain laws of income-tax arithmetic, plus certain conditions pertaining to your particular income bracket. But if you were to ask an electronics engineer what determined the behavior of that computer and allow him to lift the lid and look inside, he would tell you a physical story, not a mathematical one: he'd say the behavior of that mass of transistors was determined by the laws of physics as applied to the copper and whatnot in its components. His determination of behavior at that level is complete in terms of the laws of physics—but nobody with any sense would suggest that this rules out the claims of the income-tax inspector.

The same logical point applies, I suggest, to our choosing as determining our behavior, *vis-a-vis* the physical story that a physicist or a physiologist might be able to tell about the determination of the processes inside our heads. Just as it is illogical to conclude that the two different descriptions of the computer couldn't both be true, it is illogical to conclude that if there were a complete physical explanation of what determined the processes inside my head, then I couldn't be held to have determined my behavior by my choices. It simply doesn't follow.

Assume, for the sake of argument, that all that you believe and know and feel and think is represented in some sense by the physical configuration of your brain. I have shown elsewhere (for example, in *Brains, Machines and Persons*) that even if that configuration were fully mechanistic in its workings, no complete specification of your brain would exist that you would be bound to accept as inevitable, unless the specification were of its past. In particular, no complete specification of the immediate future of your brain could have an unconditional claim to your assent, even if your brain were as mechanical as the workings of a clock.

The reason for this, of course, is that if all your mental processes are represented in your brain, then no change can take place in any mental state of yours without a change also taking place in the physical state of your brain. And therefore the validity of any complete specification of your brain depends on whether or not you believe it. So it doesn't have an unconditional claim to your assent. No matter how clever I might be in preparing the specification, it can't be equally correct whether or not you believe it. If I accurately describe the make-up of your brain at the moment you read or hear my description, it will be incorrect by the time you've accepted its truth, because the simple act of acquiescence will have changed your brain's make-up. Alternatively, if I can allow for the effects of your believing the description, so as to produce one that you would be correct to believe, then its correctness will *depend* on your believing it—so you would not be mistaken to disbelieve it!

In that sense, then, the immediate future of your brain is open to *you*, undetermined for *you*, and would remain so even if the physical elements making up your brain were as determinate as the solar system. There isn't time to say more about this, but I think it is an important point to recognize: that in order to defend the responsibility of ourselves and our fellow men for our choices, we don't even have to argue—let alone prove—

that there must be some gap in the chains of cause and effect in our brains that the scientist might look for.[3]

Let me emphasize that although we've talked about "deterministic" science and we've imagined powers of prediction to the nth degree, the fact is that human science, being a limited enterprise, is always tentative. But what I have been arguing is that there is no need for people (particularly Christians) who cherish human dignity and the meaningfulness of life to cherish the gaps that do exist in the explanatory structure of natural science. In particular there is no need for us to oppose the scientific approach to the study of man. There is, I think, some truth in Nietzsche's remark that science dethrones man, but I suggest that the thrones that science can remove him from are those which he had no business occupying in the first place.

[3]Note that this argument offers no objection to the possibility that a *detached non-participant* (an "ideal observer" who sees all but cannot interfere) might know in advance what you will in fact believe, and hence what state your brain will lie in, at some future time. The point is that what *he* would be correct to believe about it is something *you* would be mistaken (in detail) to believe if you knew it (for the reasons I have outlined); so it could have no unconditional claim to *your* assent, even though it had an unconditional claim to *his* assent. There is an inescapable element of *relativity* here. Where future descriptions of human actions are in question, "claims to assent" can be quite different for different individuals. An "ideal observer" may correctly see as inevitable for *him* a future action which is not at all inevitable for *you*, if you are the one who has to decide the action. You would actually be mistaken to believe what he would be correct to believe about it, until you have made up your mind.

Here we make contact with a main strand in the thinking of Pascal himself. His greatest concern was that we should give up all our bogus claims to greatness as human beings so that we could reckon realistically with our true greatness as creatures of God, called to know and love our Creator and to become members of His family. He made it clear how little greatness we can claim for ourselves:

> What a chimera then is man; what a novelty; what a chaos; what a compound of inconsistencies; a judge of all things, yet a feeble earthworm; a depository of truth, yet a heap of uncertainty; the glory and the outcast of the universe. If he magnifies himself I abase him; if he abases himself I magnify him; and persist in contradicting him till he admit that he is an incomprehensible monster.[4]

Actually, however, Pascal is not as harsh and grim as he sounds here. Let me quote from another of his thoughts on religion and philosophy:

> I blame equally those who make it their sole business to extol man, and those who take it on them to blame him and those also who attempt to amuse him. I can approve none but those who examine his nature with sorrow and compassion. It is dangerous to show man in how many respects he resembles the lower animals, without pointing out his grandeur. It is also dangerous to direct his attention to his grandeur

[4]Blaise Pascal, *Thoughts on Religion & Philosophy*, trans. Isaac Taylor (Edinburgh: John Grant, 1894), p. 46.

without keeping him aware of his degradation. It is still more dangerous to leave him ignorant of both; but to exhibit both to him will be most beneficial.[5]

## SCIENCE: NO ENEMY OF MEANING

What I've been arguing, then, is that although a few individual scientists and their followers may have sparked the notion that science is out to destroy meaning, this notion has in fact been based on a confusion. For its limited purposes science may systematically ignore the meaning of what it studies, but it has no grounds whatsoever for denying that meaning. The scientist tries, in principle, to make his descriptions exhaustive in their own terms on their own level. But this doesn't in the least mean that he is trying to exclude or invalidate descriptions at other levels whose meaning may in fact be even more important.

It follows that those who rightly want to defend the meaningfulness of human life have no rational incentive to denigrate science as such. This applies particularly, I suggest, to the defense of the Christian faith and the particular claims made by it. Ours is declared to be a created world. I've already indicated that believing this declaration doesn't involve us in any need to fight scientific theories of its created past, whatever their form. The question is simply one of fact: What past has God created? But whatever is true about it, whether discovered by scientific method or any other method, is, from the biblical point of view, one of God's facts. It is to Him

[5]Pascal, *Thoughts on Religion & Philosophy*, pp. 6-7.

above all that we owe the duty to do full justice to the way He has made things.

This includes doing full justice to the uncertainties as well as the certainties. But Christians in particular should beware of over-stressing these uncertainties and giving the impression that it is the uncertainty of science that allows religion to survive. On the other hand, I've suggested that we have to beware of what has been called "scientism"—the illicit imposing of an imported meaning on science, a meaning which then pretends to the prestige of science itself. "Evolutionism" is a case in point. The biological theory of evolution, I've been suggesting, is theologically neutral, but to personify Evolution with a capital "E," as a kind of idol which can act, is to commit a solecism from a scientific point of view. It is to go out on a limb with no scientific backing whatsoever.

## SCIENCE AS AN EXPRESSION
## OF RELIGIOUS OBEDIENCE

So finally, our question: Can science and technology provide an answer to the quest for meaning? My answer, as you can see, is ultimately "No." I don't, on the other hand, think they do anything to destroy the meaning or the mystery of our world when properly understood; and they do, I suggest, enlarge our understanding. They give fresh material for our wonder—and, the Christian would say, for our worship of the Creator. On ultimate questions of the meaning of the whole show, however, they are systematically silent, because these are not scientific questions. But—and this is the point—the fact that they are not scientific questions doesn't mean that they are improper questions for the scientist or anyone else to ask as a human being. It means only that if they are to be answered, the answers will have to come from outside the system within which the game of science is defined. It's like chess-playing. If someone says, "Let's play chess," and someone else asks, "Why?" a question has arisen that the rules of chess are not framed to answer.

What I've tried to show, in particular, is that Christian theism is far from being an enemy of science: it actually offers the most rational basis for the practice of science as but one aspect of the obedience that the Creator requires of us and our world. There is no question of having to isolate Christianity from science in order to maintain peace between them. Rather, I suggest, they belong together as naturally as root and fruit: there is in principle an organic unity between biblical Christian faith and natural science.

## Discussion

QUESTION 1:
*I would like your response to the true mysteries of the Incarnation and the Crucifixion. I have my literary versions of them, but I'd like to hear your scientific versions.*

MACKAY:
I don't think there is a specifically scientific version, because the mysteries you're speaking of are given us as part of God's effort to rescue us from our state of rebel-

lion against Him, aren't they? And this is above all a participatory situation; the scientist can't stand outside of it, detached. So it's not clear to me that there is any specifically scientific story to tell there. If you mean, do I imagine that if the scientist had been there, he might have had an explanation of what happened at the resurrection of Christ, for instance, then I can only give you as an opinion—and it's worth no more than that—that I don't think he would have. In other words, I'm not one of those people so anxious to defend the universality of scientific law that I insist that there must be a scientific explanation of what happened when the tomb was found empty. I'll be saying a little about miracle in the next lecture, but I think the biblical concept of miracle is not at all one of chaos, but reflects rather the prerogative of the author over his story.

From the biblical point of view, if the author of our story wants a particular event to take a particular form, then he has only to say so, and it does. In that sense there is no difficulty or problem, as I see it, in the way of believing that God brought Jesus Christ to life again, just literally. I'm not saying that has to be what it all means, though it seems to me to be the obvious interpretation. But as a scientist I can't see that I can raise any objection to this occurrence, because science is concerned with the codification of precedent, and tells me what I ought to expect on the basis of precedent. But if there were, as Christianity claims, one totally unprecedented event right at the focus of the drama that God has created—namely, the appearance of Himself in

Christ, and the crucifixion of Christ—then as a scientist I have no precedent to go on in order to say what I would expect to happen as a result of Christ's being crucified. And if the record says that what actually happened was that the disciples found that the tomb couldn't hold Him, then as a scientist my mouth is sealed. It's certainly not necessary to scrounge around in the basement of science to find some occult *law* to explain it, because it doesn't claim to be an event with precedent.

QUESTION 2:
*Can't you see it just as a metaphor?*

MACKAY:
Well, it's at least metaphor—but metaphor can have a historical base, too, as I'm sure you would agree.

QUESTION 3:
*Could you say more about this business of "levels"?*

MACKAY:
I think most of us work at several levels. A typical example in the early days of air travel was the stewardess who weighed you first, treating you as a mass with a certain weight, and then talked to you as a passenger. And we ourselves, surely, in eating and other activities are operating at several levels. So there is nothing magical about levels: no special operation or special gift is required to move from one to the other—we do it all the time. Indeed, I think a much more difficult exercise is to discipline ourselves not to jump levels, but to really stick to

one level consistently so that we don't get trapped in some of these pseudo-problems I was detailing.

For example, people often think that it sounds logical to say, "But if the activity of my brain cells is determined by physical laws, then I can't help what I do." But in fact this involves a jump of levels, because brain cells belong to the story level of the physical brain, and an individual's choice belongs to the "I" story, the inside-agency story, which is at a different logical level. So these levels—which, remember, are meant to be a very common-sensical notion that is illustrated by the two levels in the computer—are something that we very easily slide between in our everyday discourse. And it is a more difficult problem, I think, to be systematic in sticking to one than to bridge them.

QUESTION 4:
*Looking at the scientific revolution, especially during the time of Copernicus, one can see that all major scientific research has had enormous trouble with the Church. How do you reconcile this?*

MACKAY:
Well, let me point out two things. First, on the question of fact, I didn't say that there hadn't been conflicts. I said that, fundamentally, the starting-point of modern science was biblical. But, of course, none of us would deny that there have been conflicts in the notorious cases of Galileo and Darwin and other individuals whose theories angered certain theologians; and there have been strong battles. The question, though—

when we look with hindsight at the Church's battle with Galileo, for example—is whether objections raised by the Church were a working out of the fundamental principles of the faith, or whether the Church was, in fact, grafting onto those fundamental principles presuppositions which had no base in the biblical faith. And I think it is now generally recognized that, although the theologians who quoted Psalm 96 against Galileo—"The earth is fixed so that it shall not be moved"—were undoubtedly pious men who felt they were being obedient to Scripture, when we read Psalm 96 today, we find it absurd to suggest that its function was to teach something about the astronomical fixity of the earth; Psalm 96 talks about the faithfulness of God. But, although there have been conflicts—and they haven't been nearly as universal as your question suggests—there is a large and honorable tradition of great scientists, including Boyle and Newton and Faraday and Clerk Maxwell, with important new ideas, who were themselves Christians and were never embroiled in anything like the Galileo controversy.

I think you will find that such controversies as have arisen come down to questions of interpretation of peripheral elements in the Bible, and not at all to a confrontation between the basic biblical theistic doctrine of the natural world and the practice of science to which, to some extent, it gave rise. I'm not aware of any instance in which you could say, "Ah, well, that means that Christianity, as distinct from an interpretation of a biblical text, was wrong." Let's put it this way: if the biblical theist is right in seeing science, when it's at its best, as a result of being obedient to data given by God, then to speak of science as "correcting God's Word" would be a contradiction in terms, because the data of science, as distinct from our *theories*, are from God just as much as anything else that claims to be God's Word.

QUESTION 5:
*Do you believe that science can correct the Bible?*

MACKAY:
The most that scientific discovery can do, based on God's data, is to correct *our interpretation* of what we thought God's Word was. And I think there are historical cases in which people's interpretation of the Bible has been corrected—or at least qualified and rendered less dogmatic—by data given by God through scientific discovery. But I'm not aware of any case where there has actually been an irreconcilable conflict traceable to theistic doctrine as distinct from people's idiosyncratic interpretation of it.

QUESTION 6:
*Dr. MacKay, you speak of science being a fine discipline, and you disagree with Roszak's objections to science and, I would suppose, with those of other writers such as the Christian Jacques Ellul. But these men criticize science not so much on the philosophical level as on the practical level. They point out that science has become connected to our economy and to the social structure in a way which has very harmful effects on us all every day. These considerations seem much more serious than the philosophical ones you speak of.*

MacKay:

Well, I agree that there are serious things to criticize. The question is, though, whether it's proper to say that these are criticisms of science or even of technology as such. They are proper criticisms of the use that particular political groups make of scientific and technological advances. I'll be saying a bit more about this in the next lecture, because I feel rather sad about Jacques Ellul. I know he is a Christian, and he is doing, I think, a faithful job as a prophet, prophesying against misapplication of science and technology. He's very mistrustful of the way in which technology can feed arrogance in man, can nourish the arrogant attitude of independence of God and defiance of God and domination over others, which is the very reverse of the Christian image of a true human being. All this one can only applaud.

But the question is, What is the target? And I think it's confusing and most unfortunate that Ellul at least allows himself to be interpreted as saying that the target is science—or, more specifically for Ellul, technology. Technology, I'll be arguing, is the art of trying to be an efficient steward—no more than that. Technology is the art of trying to be efficient in the pursuit of ends. The basic question is not, Is the science good? or, Is the technology good? but, Are the ends good? And while I quite agree that very often the technologist is paid by the people who have ends that are not good, nevertheless it's vital, if we're going to keep our thinking straight, that we shouldn't blur the distinction between science and technology and the ends which the human race devises for them.

# The Meaning of Science

EARLIER I mentioned Thomas Gradgrind, Dickens' memorable caricature in *Hard Times*. Gradgrind was "a man of facts and calculations," reckoned to be a realist; and all of us agree, in one of our moods at least, that it's important to be realistic—particularly to be realistic in education. But what does being realistic mean? Well, I suppose by using the word we are pointing to the belief that our world, the reality that confronts us, has a structure to be reckoned with. And *reckoning*, a very central part of human agency, can be parceled out into three aspects, at least for our purposes here.

First of all there is what we call reasoning, intellect, knowledge of facts. Secondly, there is the aspect of planning and the development of techniques based on knowledge of laws. Thirdly, there is evaluating and the choice of ends, based on the recognition of values. So, as a mnemonic device we can remember facts, techniques, and ends (or values).

Now, there is a temptation, I think—and this is indeed what Dickens is obviously warning against—to imagine that being realistic means starting with the first two (facts and techniques) and letting the third (the question of ends and values) settle itself. And at this point, as we all know, biblical Christianity characteristically says, "No, this turns priorities upside-down. Seek first the Kingdom of God and His righteousness, and all these things shall be added unto you." In other words, if you want to be truly realistic, start by getting your priorities straight, and the other things will follow in a way that won't foul up the final outcome.

## IS THERE ROOM FOR SCIENCE?

It's just at this point that I think the Gradgrinds of the world, and indeed many others who wish to be more sensitive than the Gradgrind of the caricature, might raise an objection. They might say, "No doubt the teachings of Jesus Christ and the priorities at the moral level which He set before us are marvelous, if we can live up to them. No doubt the world would be a better place if we followed them through; but where in this view of the world does science fit in? Would there be room for a scientific approach? Or, conversely, does the scientific approach leave any room for the God that Jesus Christ spoke of?"

Now, I believe that the true answer to this question is that, both logically and historically, science in our modern sense finds its greatest encouragement in the biblical doctrine of the natural world as God's creation. On this subject, as regards the history of science, I can't recommend anything more highly than a paperback, by Professor R. Hooykaas of Utrecht, called *Religion and the Rise of Modern Science*. This book gives an excellent summary of the part played by biblical insights in the thinking of the founders of modern science, at the time, say, of the founding of the Royal Society in the seventeenth century. Hooykaas has summarized the thrust of his argument as follows:

> What the Bible urges upon Man is a complete transformation in his relations to God and his fellow creatures and to the world which God has made. This transformation means a liberation from all superstitious bonds as well as a new allegiance; that is, a liberation from any kind of idolatry, including the idols of "common opinion," and "official doctrine." He who has been touched by the Spirit may respect human authorities in church, state, or science, but he will not let himself be so deeply impressed by [any of] them as to give up his independence because of the weight of the "majority" or of "tradition." Not that this must be allowed to become another variety of idolatry, the idolatry of self-worship. The new liberation implies also a new obedience, by which man must be willing to commit all his prejudices and all his prior criteria of "reasonableness" to the test of divine revelation, including the facts with which he is confronted in the universe around him. . . . Thus confidence in the possibilities of science and in the freedom of thought, as well as [self-discipline] in theorizing and obedience to the dictates of nature, are the necessary consequences of a truly Biblical religion.[6]

If I may, let me spend a little time spelling out what I think is meant by this kind of claim, which is certainly

[6]R. Hooykaas, *Christian Faith & the Freedom of Science* (London: Tyndale Press, 1957), pp. 14-15.

one that I would want to advance myself. Let's look just at one or two "headings," as it were, where we see an interface between the biblical Christian doctrine of the natural world and the practice of science. First in importance—and you will find this particularly in the writings of Francis Bacon—is the emphasis on man as a steward of the created order, who will be held accountable to God. In other words, the concept of stewardship provides a primary motivation for getting out there and seeing what can be done with the created order for the benefit of our fellow men. That incentive is appealed to again and again by the early writers, who promote it over against the scholastic tradition, in defense of the experimental approach to natural science.

Then, secondly (and this, to me, is perhaps the key to the whole problem of relating constructively and integrally the Christian religious doctrine of the natural world and the scientific approach), there is the emphasis that you find in both the Old and the New Testament— made very explicit in the New Testament— on the dynamic nature of the dependence of our world on God.

## DYNAMIC STABILITY

Let me illustrate the sort of thing I mean. You find, for example, the writer to the Hebrews speaking of God as "upholding all things [present tense] by His word of power." And you might very well wonder, as I certainly did for many years, what on earth was needed by way of upholding. Here is a room with a perfectly good, solid floor and roof. The roof is upheld by the pillars—what kind of upholding is left to be done by the alleged Creator? But there is nowadays a simple illustration that helps me to make sense of what is being said here, one that relates very well to the kind of thinking that the scientist does. I'm referring to the kind of device that you can buy now in the toy stores to attach to your television set, which produces on the screen a created world of events. You know what I mean—you can set the thing up to play tennis, for example, and on your television screen a little ball moves back and forth between courts and is struck by facsimiles of racquets. You can either play a game with yourself or play with somebody else.

If you look at it from the physical point of view, this world on the TV screen is actually held in being by the stability of a program of events—namely, the impact of electrons on the screen. If you examine any point closely, you find a continual rattle of electrons giving rise to a continual sparkle of light which maintains in being the objects and activities that you're watching. Every object on the screen has its being in and through this continuing, coherent pattern of events, so that somebody equipped with a suitable box of this sort can be described as the creator of a world in which certain things happen according to regular laws. If we want to make the illustration a little more to the point, we can imagine that the device isn't equipped with a lot of computing operations; instead, it's got some sort of keyboard on which you've got to work very fast, and by doing so you can, if you will, bring into being a ball and a racquet and the sequence of events in which they interact.

Now, if you were to do this kind of thing as a creator, then the extent to which your little world would be worth studying by a scientist would depend on the extent to which you are prepared to maintain a coherent pattern of precedent, wouldn't it? I mean, if you are so minded, then every time the ball hits the racquet at a given angle it will rebound at a corresponding angle, which can be predicted from the measurement of the initial angle, and so forth. There will be, in other words, *laws of motion* in the world of your television screen which reflect the stability of your creative purpose. Of course, if you were not so minded, then there would be no laws of motion worth trying to discover, because at one time the impact would produce one sort of rebound, and perhaps at another time the ball would just disappear, according to your whim. This capriciousness would bring into being a world on that screen that wasn't worth a scientist's attention.

## SCIENTIFIC LAWS

But a creator who had a coherent pattern of precedent, according to which he wanted the events on the screen to occur, would be the sort of creator whose works would be rewarding for what we nowadays call the "scientific approach," revealing correlations of a regular kind that we could describe as "laws." The objects in the world would have no inherent stability independent of their creator. They would, of course, be stable for as long as he was willing to "uphold" them—i.e., hold them in being by his creative work on the keyboard; but they wouldn't have the kind of "eternal" stability, as it were, that he himself would have relative to the events on the screen. If he were to cease his creative activity, they would disappear.

Now that is only an illustration. It is very imperfect, as any theologian, I'm sure, would want to remind me. But I think it does bring out something of what is meant by the biblical claim that our world is the creation of God, and not just in the sense that at some point in the past something unusual happened—the "big bang," ten to the tenth years ago, or whatever. It's not only that kind of claim. Indeed, no particular point in time is singled out, I would say, by the claim that God is Creator. He is the upholder now of all events that have their being, and they continue to have their being because of the stability of His upholding power, because of His creative intentions for the world in which we find ourselves. The world of objects, then, has a dynamic stability in the sense in which the objects on that TV screen have a dynamic stability. This biblical concept of our world as a world of created events, cohering according to precedent because their Creator is faithful to a pattern, positively encourages the sort of expectations that we call "scientific." They are expectations based on precedent. And science, from this point of view, can be called the "codification of precedent" with a view to the systematic organization of expectations.

In that sense, then, we could say that scientific laws are prescriptive, not merely descriptive. Those of you interested in the philosophy of science will know that there has been a good deal of debate about whether it is at all proper to describe scientific laws as prescribing what happens, rather than merely describing. I think as far as phenomena are concerned, I'm on the side of those who say that scientific laws merely describe. Newton's Laws, for example, don't *make* the planets move round the sun; they simply describe the way they move. But they do prescribe the expectations that we rationally ought to entertain on the basis of precedent. They don't guarantee that precedent must be followed; but they do insist that when precedent *is* being followed, we ought to expect certain things to happen according to the laws that have been established.

## MIRACLE

Now you might say, "This is all very well, but surely at the center of the Christian doctrine of our world is a miracle, the miracle of the resurrection of Christ. Among the many others that are described in the Bible, this one is surely central, and surely the whole concept of miracle, bringing in the idea of events that violate precedent, is anathema to the scientific spirit." Well, it's quite clear that a miracle, were it to happen, would be a shock to scientific expectations. That's one thing. But it is quite different—and, I think, false—to suggest that there is anything whatever in the scientific method or spirit or approach which requires any guarantee that a miracle has never happened, and that all events always have occurred according to precedent.

Think again of simulating a game of tennis on TV. If

you invite a scientist to study the screen, then no doubt you'll play fair with him, and unless you want to tease him, you will continue according to one pattern until he has a chance to discover what the pattern is. But, on the other hand, if there are good and sufficient reasons why at some point this pattern can't continue—for example, if it's time to stop for lunch—then the scientist doesn't suddenly complain, "You've made my whole game meaningless." The point is that you have had a different kind of reason other than mere adherence to precedent for an event which was unprecedented: namely, the disappearance of the events from the screen.

Now again, it's only a limited analogy, but I think that to the extent that, let us say, the resurrection of Christ is presented as an event without precedent, it is presented as an event which was necessary at that point in God's created drama: the One whom men had crucified was none other than the Creator himself, and it was impossible, as Peter puts it, that death should have been the end of Him. If that is the state of affairs, then the scientist who believes in this Creator, trusts Him, loves Him, and serves Him, isn't going to complain that a belief that this event occurred once without precedent makes nonsense of his game. Of course he won't—because, indeed, the resurrection of Christ is presented not as an act of caprice, not as something which is liable to happen any time and will make a fool of a scientist any day that he is trying to establish something solidly. On the contrary, it is presented as the most natural and, indeed, inevitable event required by God's faithfulness to the whole purpose of the Incarnation. In other words, it is an event coherent with the Creator's purpose, coherent at a different level from that of following precedent, but coherent nonetheless. The point I'm making is that the biblical concept of miracle is poles apart from the irrational and the capricious, the sort of thing that sends shivers down the scientist's spine.

Certainly it does mean that if the scientist believes that the Resurrection occurred in the way that the apostles told the story, he must admit that precedent was not followed. But he is required with equal firmness to recognize, if he believes what is being set before him, that what happened had a rationale, was indeed coherent, but coherent with the overall purpose of God in the redemption of man. In other words, the dynamic stability that biblical doctrine attributes to the natural world means that we have every ground for expecting that the normal pattern of events will be a pattern according to a fixed precedent, worthy of the scientist's study and reliable on the basis of scientific laws as discovered. But, on the other hand, there is no absolute guarantee against an event arriving with a note attached to it: "You didn't expect this, did you?"

I'm reminded of something that happened when I was a student at St. Andrew's during the war. A lecturer with a formidable speed of delivery had completely covered the face of one of those sash blackboards, as she did almost every day, at a speed much greater than we could write things down, and then flung up the sash to reveal the lower blackboard. On it was drawn a thirty-mile-an-hour sign with a scribbled message beneath it: "You didn't expect this, did you?" You see the point. There is absolutely nothing to prevent God, if He wished, from bringing about any pattern of unprecedented events. Nothing, that is to say, ontologically. Nothing but His own faithfulness and character, as set out in the biblical doctrine of a God who doesn't behave capriciously. A God who is trustworthy is the guarantee to the scientist that natural events will not break precedents unless God has a special reason to do so; the scientist can thus rely from day to day on his expectations based on the systematic observation of precedent which we call science.

## ACCOUNTABILITY

What, then, does science mean in this perspective? Well, it means first, and primarily, that once we have codified, and in that sense understood, the pattern of precedent in a particular field, then consequences can be foreseen, and therefore our knowledge of a limited sample gives us knowledge of much more, either of things elsewhere in the world or about the future of the situation that we are studying. The relevant point for our present purpose is that with this increased ability to foresee and to generalize comes greatly increased *accountability*. So if you asked me to define in a sentence the principal meaning of science, I would say, "The principal meaning of science is the enlargement of our accountability." According to the Bible, "To whom much is given, of him will much be required." The more you know as a result of your scientific observation of precedent, the more you are responsible for outcomes that, on the basis of precedent, you ought now to be able to foresee.

Is it a good thing, then, to know more? Might we not be better off if we didn't know it? There are some spirits of our time who would whisper—or even trumpet—that the scientist is sinning as Pandora did in her desire for knowledge. Wouldn't it be far better to know less, and be less answerable for the use we make of the knowledge? But again, the biblical answer to this from Jesus himself is surely in the parable of the talents, familiar to us all. As you remember, various people were given talents to develop, and when the allotted time was up, one wretch came cringing with his talent wrapped up in a napkin and said, in effect, "I was scared to do anything with this because of the risk of possible consequences." His master dismissed him, as a worthless and unprofitable servant, because he had dragged his feet—had failed to do what he could reasonably have been expected to do. In other words, it is no good for us to wish that we didn't have the kind of responsibility that science gives us, for the knowledge we gain from science, from the biblical point of view, is knowledge given by God. Of course we've got to do the work of observing precedent, but the data are God's data, given events which are of His making and His giving to us. He'll hold us accountable for making the fullest good use of them.

So, from the biblical standpoint, the path of responsible realism lies between two extremes. On the one hand is the extreme of heedless exploitation which, I think, is what some people have in mind when they criticize science. The exploiter of scientific discovery often fails to reckon with some of its foreseeable consequences; he is too infatuated with the immediate profits predicted from some of the more close-at-hand developments. Heedless exploitation, then, is clearly one extreme to be avoided by the responsible realist. But the other extreme that we've also got to avoid is that of the craven foot-dragger, so to speak, the man who wraps up his talent in a napkin. Stewardship, which is declared to be our responsibility in the eyes of our Creator, includes the responsibility to be efficient in the use of the talents and gifts that the Creator gives us.

## IS SCIENCE OBJECTIVE?

Now along these lines (which I think were more clearly perceived in the days of the Christian founders of modern science than they often are now), I believe we can rediscover the fullest and most harmonious possible integration of natural science within the framework of Christian faith. I won't spend time on this now, partly because I've argued it in greater detail elsewhere, particularly in *Science, Chance and Providence*. But I do want to go on to one or two questions of current debate in the philosophy of science which in the perspective of biblical theism appear in a different light—and in some ways, it seems to me, a clearer light. For instance, there is much dispute nowadays about the truth and the objectivity of scientific conclusions. Can we say that scientific theorizing and observation lead to truth in any worthwhile sense, and that science is objective? Every science has its limits, we are reminded, and that is perfectly true. Others will tell us, particularly those with certain political beliefs, that all knowledge is culturally conditioned and, therefore, the idea of objective, value-free knowledge is a myth.

Now, I have already made it clear that there are some limits to the scientific approach in any field, which will leave us bound to admit that we could be mistaken. On the other hand, the limits in some cases are so hypothetical that we would be irresponsible and dishonest if we were to pretend that we were uncertain about them—for example, if we were to feign uncertainty about the lethal potential of arsenic. It doesn't take a very sophisticated scientist to discover that; and anyone who pleaded innocent of poisoning a man with arsenic on the grounds that the outcome was unknowable, because "science is always uncertain," would probably be locked up.

So I'm suggesting that a kind of hypocrisy may tempt us when we talk about the limits of science. It's not good enough to pretend that all scientific facts are so uncertain that they can be airily dismissed by anyone who wants to be capricious. Nevertheless, it is true that our conclusions, in more speculative areas especially, are severely limited by the sampling we do; and as I'll be suggesting later, it would be good, perhaps, for the health of science if the teaching of science reflected this fact more often.

We also have to realize that in some fields, and perhaps notably in the social sciences, the *kinds* of questions a person asks about a particular field of investigation may be culturally conditioned. In other words, the questions reflect his social background, his upbringing, the books he's read, and things of that sort. He may accept these influences, or he may react against them; but one way or another, his questions are likely to be culturally conditioned. The point is not so much that an honest man asking a culturally conditioned question will come up with false information, but that he may miss vitally important information—in fact, he may miss the whole point of the situation—by not asking the right question.

You see what I mean. There are people who use the phrase "cultural conditioning," for example, when they talk about "Western capitalist science." What they imply is that from the standpoint of the philosophy of science there is something quite untrustworthy about it because it is culturally conditioned by Western ideas. You will even find people trying to argue, for example, that B. F. Skinner's behaviorism is untrustworthy because it reflects "Western capitalist" values of reward and punishment and so forth.[7] (As a matter of fact, Skinner doesn't normally use punishment.)

[7]For a balanced critique of behaviorism from a Christian standpoint, see M. A. Jeeves, *Psychology and Christianity: The View Both Ways* (London: InterVarsity Press, 1976). See also D. M. MacKay, *Human Science & Human Dignity* (London: Hodder & Stoughton, 1979).

In any case, this insistence that scientific conclusions are culturally influenced must be looked at with great care because, in general, cultural influence will simply tend to make an honest observer ask limited questions—not factually distort the discoveries he makes. Of course I'm not talking about the rare individual who will twist scientific data—misreport them and so on—for his own ends. That's something quite different and not worthy of our consideration here. But it is possible for an honest man, whether his background is Marxist or capitalist, to fail to get the point of a situation because a cultural blind spot prevents him from asking the right question. Anthropologists studying primitive tribes have been among the principal reporters—and sometimes, alas, conspicuous exemplars—of this phenomenon.

Clearly, then, there are some relativistic aspects to science as well as some clear limits to the detail and precision with which we can make scientific observations. But it seems to me that it is a mistake to suggest, as some writers in our day are doing, that this implies that the goal of value-free knowledge is an illusion, a myth, something not worth pursuing, and that the concept of scientific objectivity is outdated because of what we now know about cultural conditioning and similar factors. People who argue this way are extrapolating far beyond any conclusion justified by the data they cite.

I think the theistic perspective helps us to see just how far these particular qualifications of scientific observation and certainty fail to diminish the value of science. Take the theistic concept of God as Creator once again.

What this means in practice for the scientist who believes in God is that no matter how difficult he may find it to transcend the limits of his technique, no matter how plagued he may be by blind spots of knowledge and imagination, none of this denies that before him there stands a Judge of the truth and objectivity of any claim he makes. In other words, if there is a Creator of our world, if the whole of our world in every detail owes its being to a Creator (just as every detail in a novel owes its being to the author)—if that is the situation that we are in, as scientists, then a scientist who holds this belief must recognize that there are always objective facts about the situation, and there is a Judge who can determine, who *does* determine, the extent to which he, as a scientist, is near or far from the truth.

So objectivity, it seems to me, is integrated with the Christian concept of the natural world. Objectivity in science, however difficult it may be for us to attain, is a meaningful goal, a goal which challenges us to a measurable degree of success or failure. The measurement is made not by us, but by God—but that it is made is what the Christian scientist accepts. Scientific *judgments* may not always be value-free. Our values, our prejudices, our limitations may bias the judgments we make. But this does nothing to invalidate the concept of value-free *knowledge* as the goal and the ideal after which the scientist should strive. Like righteousness in the domain of the spirit, it is no less meaningful or valid as a goal because it is imperfectly attainable.

This, I suggest, is so, even—or especially—when particular items of knowledge may be socially or politically unpalatable. We remember, for example, the Lysenko scandal in the Soviet Union. Because an official dogma ran counter to beliefs which were shared mainly among Western scientists, Lysenko was able to suppress a good deal of scientific activity in the Soviet Union even when the scientific data being produced were solid and recognized as such. There are parallel situations today in a number of sensitive social areas that I probably don't need to specify. The danger is always there that data unpalatable to certain social or political groups will be countered with the suggestion that, since all scientists will be biased, "there's no such thing as an objective fact." And this, as a technical thesis in the practice or philosophy of science, is simply false.

What we do have to remember, though, is that although scientific facts may be value-free, the decision to communicate these facts generally is not. For example: suppose it happens to be a sad and easily established fact that an otherwise beautiful young lady has a wart on her nose. This fact, as such, is value-free. It's there whether you like it or not, however you value it. But for me to stand up at a party at which the young lady was present and loudly proclaim this as a fact would not be a value-free action at all. And I think this is true in our society about some of the more sensitive data that social science and other sciences may discover—for example, data about racial characteristics. There may be a great many things that are true (some of them already known), which, declared in a given context, could be inflammatory and far from value-free. That is to say, the declaration of them may be far from value-free even though the facts themselves are. I think this is just one other aspect of the enhanced responsibility which is part of the meaning of science.

## THE MEANING OF SCIENCE

In summary, then, what have we been suggesting that science means? First and foremost, it means an increase in our accountability; an increase in opportunities for compassionate action and the exercise of responsible foresight for the benefit of our fellow men. For example, disease is on the one hand something that may be checked by antibiotics and things of that sort, or it may be something which statistically can be checked by forms of genetic control. Energy supply is something which no doubt we can derive from solar devices and other convenient means in some locations. But countries which get less than a rich supply of solar energy, like my own Scotland, look rather dimly on the suggestion that we should turn in the future to solar energy as the replacement of, let us say, nuclear energy. Disease, energy, food supply, too—these are all examples of areas in which the mere suggestion that we should downgrade scientific investigation and turn our backs on technology would seem grossly uncompassionate and irresponsible.

Secondly, I think science means unlimited growth of our wonder and awe at the mysterious universe in which we find ourselves. I referred to this before, but I think the point is worth underscoring. Just as in the seventeenth century when this point was often emphasized, it's true today—and perhaps increasingly true—that each discovery which explains something that puzzled us also reveals something more marvelous and intricate in the structure of our universe.

Thirdly, science means the steady growth of our confidence that precedent can be a reliable guide to expectations—or, as a Christian theist would say, our confidence in the trustworthiness of the Creator who holds in being the natural world. Today we probably take this too much for granted. But we need only look back to the period before natural science developed in its modern form to see that this idea was by no means obvious then. Precedent was only a very limited guide because at that time scientists hadn't developed the procedures for so classifying precedent that they could single out one factor and say, "This is the thing that is the same in A as it was in B." So many uncontrolled factors entered in that it just didn't occur to people, even in areas that we now think we understand, that there would be a precedent worth observing.

Of course, there were some precedents they were aware of. As the book of Proverbs quaintly puts it, "Does not the ringing of the nose bring forth blood?" Recognized sequences of cause and effect were not confined to those discovered scientifically. What is new about our modern science is its technique for so isolating individual factors in a complicated situation that we're now able to identify very subtly defined precedents and say, "Given this subtle combination of circumstances, then a rather precise outcome can be expected." The increasing confidence that this is a valid way of organizing our lives is something that, from the standpoint of Christian theism, increases our reasons for thanking God for His trustworthiness.

In this sense it's clear that science can lead us to truth. But we have to remember the personal aspect of this concept of truth emphasized by the biblical writers. "I *am* the Truth" was the claim of Christ. Hooykaas, from whom I read a few moments ago, puts it this way:

> It is evident that Truth in the biblical sense is not an abstract truth but a Person, Christ, or the Spirit of Christ. So taking into account both kinds of truth, we could perhaps better say that [to the early founders of the Royal Society] it was truth [with a capital "T"] which led to the freedom necessary to find truth [with a small "t"].

Then, paraphrasing Pascal, he concludes: "We cannot be radically free until, tired and exhausted from the vain search after truth, we have stretched our arms to the Liberator."

## THE TEMPTATIONS OF THE SCIENTIST

Now, having said all this, I've left unmentioned a very important qualification. We mustn't forget—because there is plenty of evidence for it—that science also means a growing temptation to become proud and engage in self-centered exploitation and domination. It's only natural, if a man's goal is exploitation, that each

[8]Hooykaas, *Christian Faith & the Freedom of Science*, p. 23.

discovery of science is seen first as an increase of his power in the relevant area. Now, I'm not one of those who preaches that power is necessarily a bad thing. Power, as I've been suggesting indirectly, is an increase in responsibility, and of itself to be judged good or bad according to the way we use it. But it is clear in our world of mixed motives that it would be quite unrealistic to neglect the strength with which scientific resources appeal to our pride and desire for domination—which raises, finally, the awkward question of whether there is any remedy for this danger. This brings me back to the three aspects of realistic reckoning that we summarized at the beginning. You remember there were reasoning and facts to be reckoned with, planning and techniques to be taken into account, and evaluation and the choice of ends to consider. And it is of course in the third area that science as such is powerless (though its data are important), and that we have our greatest difficulty as a society in determining the ends to be pursued.

In the last analysis, science and technology are worse than useless unless our society is *morally* realistic in selecting the ends to which these shall be applied. It's a matter of concern to many serious thinkers in our day, and certainly not exclusively to Christians, that so little attention is given to this aspect of realistic education in our universities. Let me quote, for example, some ideas on the subject from Sir Eric Ashby:

> Our system of higher education, which has been the formal apprenticeship for most of the technological

goal-setters ... gives no training in two essential areas: for politicians and administrators there is no training in how to use the inputs of science in the making of political decisions; for scientists there is no training in how to give due weight to non-cognitive considerations in choosing extrinsic goals for science. When, for example, do the results of science justify political action? Should cigarettes be as illegal as pot? Should women in overcrowded countries be obliged to take the pill under risk of punishment, as some units of Australian soldiers were obliged during the war in New Guinea to take Atebrin against malaria? Should air-lines pay through airport charges for the noise pollution they cause, and the proceeds be used to provide double-glazing in all homes within ten miles of the runway? These are the sorts of questions which cannot be answered within the framework of science alone or politics alone. Neither the scientist nor the politician can get from our system of higher education an expertise for dealing with such questions.[9]

Professor Hooykaas in another paper makes a related point when writing about the Christian approach to teaching science. "Not personal power and money-making," he says, "but the glory of God and the well-being of mankind ought to be our motives in seeking to extend our power over nature. Moreover, it should be made clear [in the teaching of science] by concrete examples that an unlimited exercise of our scientific and technological power leads to disaster and is illicit,

[9]Sir Eric Ashby, "Science and Antiscience," *Sociological Review Monograph*, 18 (1972), 209-226, especially 216-217.

not"—and this is important—"not because God reserves certain parts of the world for Himself, but because man has been made a steward over his fellow creatures and is not allowed to deal with them in an irresponsible way." He says we have to steer clear of "an archaistic, reactionary defense of relics of Pagan nature worship in Christian disguise," to avoid investigating nature fearfully, as if it were a kind of Pandora's box. The middle course lies between this approach and the progressivist hubris of modern scientism, "between a feeble submission to nature and a belief in infinite progress achievable through pulling ourselves up by our own bootlaces in over-confidence in our own intellect and our own power."[10]

Now even though these are clear and stirring words, it's obvious that there is no easy solution to this problem of teaching realistic evaluation of the applications of science—even more so, of course, in what is nowadays called a "pluralistic society." But I suggest that there is no more urgently important problem for our society to tackle by the coming together of people of good will from all persuasions. We need a commitment to seek urgently to remedy the present chaotic condition, in which virtually nothing is said in our many courses in science and technology that would help the practitioners to value more realistically the final application of

---

[10]R. Hooykaas, *The Christian Approach in Teaching Science* (London: Tyndale Press, 1960), p. 19.

their skills. "For what shall it profit a man [or a society] if he gain the whole world and lose his own soul?"

Can we realistically expect that the drift away from Christian values in our society can be reversed? Much depends on whether you believe that God is there to be reckoned with and is ultimately still in control. One of the stark tragedies of the past century, I believe, is the way in which a distorted image of science and technology has been used by the enemies of religion to persuade people that, as moderns, they couldn't continue to believe in the God who revealed Himself in Jesus Christ. I do not believe, any more than Pascal did, that scientific findings can be used to prove the existence of God. I believe that He has His own way of making Himself known as a reality to be reckoned with by those of us who are ready for the consequences. But I hope that the kind of analysis that we've carried through in these lectures may help to make clear that no rational obstacle to Christian faith is offered by scientific knowledge. The invitation and challenge in the historic Christian gospel is as fully open to us today as it was in any previous age.[11]

Perhaps I might end with a word of encouragement from the philosopher H. H. Price, written a few decades ago. "The sense of the Divine," he says, "is repressed in

[11]I have elaborated some of the arguments summarized here in three other books: *Science, Chance & Providence* (New York: Oxford University Press, 1978); *Human Science & Human Dignity* (London: Hodder & Stoughton, 1979); *Brains, Machines & Persons* (London: William Collins Sons, 1980; Grand Rapids, Michigan: Eerdmans, 1980).

the minds of many people today, but not forever. The time will come when our modern, naturalistic outlook will seem topsy-turvy, a systematic attempt to put second things first and first things nowhere."

# Discussion

QUESTION 1:
*You say that science leads us to truth with a small t, or operational truth. Do I understand you correctly, that you agree with Hooykaas on this point?*

MACKAY:
Yes, though I qualify it, following Hooykaas, by saying that the road to truth with a small *t* is confidence in the lawfulness of things; and the Christian goes by way of Him who is the Truth with a capital *T* because it is through Him as Creator, and His faithfulness, that we have a rational basis for our confidence in the truth (with a small *t*) of our predictions, and liberation from our rationalistic prejudices.

QUESTION 2:
*Could I elaborate on this point? Rather than use the word truth, which I think muddies the issues, could we consider the word knowledge? Four centuries ago we had some clearly defined concepts of knowledge. We had epistémē in a Greek form, or scientific knowledge, which referred to the arts and crafts, indicating a mundane or secular knowledge. Then there was the word gnόsis, with the theological connotations of absolute truth, a higher truth which you would call Christian truth. That distinction was obscured in the post-Galileo*

*period. But now once again in the twentieth century we find scientists like yourself saying that science is perhaps strictly epistémē. Do you believe that a scientific concept can be considered a theological or gnostic concept? In other words, can we, through scientific concepts, build a Christian theology?*

MACKAY:

No. It does not follow from anything I have been saying that through scientific observation and evaluation of the data we should reach any conclusions about the giver of the data, except in the general sense which Paul hints at in writing to the Romans—that God's power and His faithfulness, if once we consider Him to exist, are exhibited by the regularities. But to anyone who says, watching that television screen, "I can do my science without reference to the person creating the objects on the screen," my answer would have to be, "Yes, of course you can, because the Creator is not one of the objects on the screen. The objects have their being in and through the activity of the Creator, but he is not visible as one of the objects." Analogously, I think that people attempting to use scientific data to make a proof for the existence of God—or, indeed, anything else about God—apart from biblical revelation about Him, are backing a loser. Pascal says this, too.

QUESTION 3:
*A number of schools of thought, one being "process theology," state that scientific concepts form a logical and rational basis for theology. Would you comment?*

MacKay:

You cannot pretend that our thoughts about God are separable from our knowledge of the world that God has made. So our knowledge of the world, including our scientific knowledge, may qualify or give content to theological affirmations about Him. For instance, Jesus talks about God sending His rain upon the just and the unjust. These are scientific facts, and you could say, "Well, Jesus is making a theological point by indicating a scientific fact." But He is not. What He is really saying is, "We all know that the rain falls, but look, what it means is that the Creator is willing to be good to all men, no matter how rebellious they are against Him." So the specifically theological point comes and builds, not by deduction from the scientific fact *qua* scientific, but upon the experience of people, which can be codified scientifically on the one hand, and on the other hand has its moral dimension. In other words, I think Jesus is saying, "The human race should be grateful to the Creator for being so evenhanded in the way that He supplies the rain."

Now I think this declaration illustrates, on the one hand, that scientifically establishable data are not irrelevant to theology, and yet, on the other hand, that the specifically theological content of affirmations has to come from the Creator if we are going to have any knowledge of them. I am certainly not sympathetic to those who imagine that ideas about the Creator can be proved by purely scientific observation. You can regard them as illustrative of concepts the Creator has already revealed, but not as a satisfactory basis for deduction *a priori*.

QUESTION 4:
*Do you feel that in the last three or four hundred years our willingness to take scientific facts and draw conclusions from them has increased? For example, if someone today argued that the earth did actually rotate around the sun, but had no evidence, would he not be laughed at today just as Galileo was laughed at hundreds of years ago? Do you think we are any more ready to accept inspiration in our scientists than we were in Galileo's day?*

MACKAY:
We always think we know what common sense is, and we resist ideas that seem to lack it. And, therefore, I don't doubt that there are situations today in which scientific discovery may be resisted, as the discovery of the motion of the earth was resisted, on the ground that it seems to violate common sense. A typical recent example would be the principle of uncertainty as applied to electrons, or Einstein's theory of relativity. For a time these were both resisted in the name of common sense or scientific tradition by a number of quite distinguished scientists. So if that is what you mean—yes, I think the human race is still often blinded by habit and custom.

But I don't think we should be too superior about this scepticism, because it is a sound principle, one which keeps science healthy and free of cranks and time-wasters by resisting change unless there is good solid evidence justifying it. No one is a greater pest in science than the man who says, "I'm tired of taking this for granted; let's try doubting it." What the scientific community says to him is, "Give us evidence; show us an observation that is inconsistent with it and we'll publish it gladly. But don't just waste our time by saying, 'Suppose one day this were to happen?' That is not a scientific question until you've got something to anchor it to."

As I said, I don't suppose that for all the philosophy of science we have lost much of our tendency to initially resist new concepts. But I don't think we'd have better science if we removed all resistance to novel ideas. A healthy scepticism keeps science sanitary, keeps the bugs out.

QUESTION 5:
*Truth, you say, is not necessarily tainted by culture. However, I wonder if it is tainted by our methods of observation? The kinds of experiments we do determine what we see. For example, to use a thermometer to measure the temperature of a fluid changes the temperature we are attempting to measure. Some people speak of the bootstrap theory, which seems antithetical to what you are saying, for it argues that the structure of nature depends on how we look at it, that there is no external truth, but only our constructs. Maybe this is self-conceit. But I wonder how you would respond. That approach seems closer to other religious traditions than to Christian religious tradition.*

MACKAY:
There are, as you say, limits imposed on science by our methods of examination. In some areas of science there

are serious limits to the precision with which we can arrive at reliable knowledge, or in your sense, truth. The area of sub-atomic physics is one. Physics has had to accept a "principle of uncertainty" according to which no complete determination of the prior state of an electron will fully determine its subsequent behavior. But this doesn't mean that what you arrive at is not true; it simply means that what you arrive at is uncertain. You can still make a true statement about the nature and degree of that uncertainty. That is what quantum theory tries to do. It uses a wave model in which the height of the wave, roughly speaking, represents the probability of a particular kind of event occurring in the region where you are measuring it. So you get a measure of probability instead of a precise prediction. But the question still arises, "Have you got the right wave function, or have you got the wrong one?" In other words, you've got to be right or wrong, and in that sense questions of truth do come up.

When it comes to human science, we encounter another kind of limit. As I argued earlier, no completely detailed, predictive description of a human being can be claimed to be true, regardless of who believes it. So that is a whole area in which the nature of knowledge changes from a spectator's knowledge to a relational knowledge of a peculiar sort. Nothing I've said is meant to deny that. That is another of the limits of science to which I have referred. But you can still say that there are true things and false things to be said about other people. So I'm not in the least claiming that there is a final proposition to be uttered about every state of the world such that anyone who believes it will be correct. That would be exactly contrary to what I've argued in print elsewhere. But I am saying that the scientific approach is an attempt to be as precise as we can about things that are objectively the case, whether we like them or not. There are some things which don't have that character of like-it-or-not, and the state of your brain one moment from now is one of them. What makes us responsible for our actions is that not even the most complete physical observation of our brain can generate a full specification of its immediate future which we would be correct to believe and mistaken to disbelieve.

In short, I'm agreeing that observation can sometimes interfere with accurate description, but I don't think this denies the claim that the aim of the scientist is to be as precise as possible about what is objectively true, whether he likes it or not. There will be some areas in which he is limited, and won't be able to achieve that aim. Of course there are areas in which we can and must gain our knowledge by means other than the scientific approach. But still, the Christian scientist believes there is a Creator before whom he is making his investigations, and that Creator knows what the scientist would be correct to believe about the situation, even if in relativistic situations it is necessarily different from what others would be correct to believe. The Creator is the arbiter of whether we are correctly doing our scientific job to the best of our ability. That was the point I was trying to make.

QUESTION 6:
*The law of entropy, which says that the universe is running down and shouldn't really exist as it is—would you say that this is an example of the upholding power of the Creator?*

MACKAY:
I don't think I'd want to single that out particularly. You see, rightly or wrongly, I interpret the law of entropy as reducible to the proposition that for any system in an established state, you can only increasingly lose track if the system is closed to you. In other words, any system in a given state, left in an enclosure by itself, can only become a system less clearly defined, less certainly specifiable by you. I call it the inevitability of losing track of a closed system. That is how it works out in relation to the theory of steam engines. There are other ways of framing it, but however you do it, it is only a generalization about the statistics of the pattern of events that God holds in being. And it doesn't point in any special way to God as the upholder. Nor does it, as I see it, take away any credibility from the claim that God is the holder-in-being of all events.

Think of the analogy of the television screen. Suppose that, as a very nimble-fingered artist, you were able to operate the keyboard in such a way as to sketch into being a world of molecules in motion in a thermodynamic environment. You could, as creator, bring about whatever pattern you wished. But if you were the creator, if you were following the principles of the Creator of our world, then presumably the particles would move in such a way that from an initially more ordered state they would gradually become more disordered—just as a triangle of billiard balls on a table, when hit by a ball, move from a neatly arranged state into a less neatly arranged state. Now, none of this would have any bearing one way or the other on the thesis that there has to be a creator at the keyboard to keep the world in motion, whether in lawful or any other kind of behavior. So I'd say that there is no special relevance of the second law to that thesis.

QUESTION 7:
*You say that from your scientific method you can only know truth with a small t. How can we be sure that we can know the truth with a capital T.*

MACKAY:
Well, I was not addressing myself to that issue in this discussion, but let me say a little about what I understand to be the New Testament's invitation to get to know Truth with a capital *T*, if you want to put it that way. As I see it, Christ is appealing to a kind of scientific spirit in us when He says, "If any man is willing to do the will of my Father, he will come to know of my teaching, whether it is from God or whether it's of my own inventing." That's one of His famous sayings, and there are others, all of which invite us, in a sense, to make an experiment. The making of this experiment requires us to face His claims and ask ourselves, "If I knew these claims were true and valid claims on my service, my priorities, and so on, would I be ready for the consequences?"

Now that is not something to be quickly answered. It

is a program to be thought through, and eventually prayed through, as the Christian would say. And for the person who becomes a Christian along the way, the outcome of that "experiment," in which he is a participant, not a detached observer, is very often this: he discovers that God does indeed take him at his word. According to Christ's promise he finds that his priorities are being reshaped, even if he doesn't live up to them perfectly, as indeed no Christian would claim he does. Despite his shortcomings, his priorities are being reshaped—if you like, he's being given "a new heart." This means something very down-to-earth at the psychological and moral level. And it's along these lines that I believe Christians find that according to Christ's promise they have begun to know the Truth. Knowing the Truth means both knowing the truth of His promises in practice, and coming to know Him as the giver of His promises. So conventionally this is spelled as Truth with a capital *T*.

I hope that is making some sense. What I'm suggesting is that the knowledge of God that is relevant for the purposes of the Christian gospel is the knowledge that comes from letting Him re-shape your priorities. And in that sense, if you come to know Him who is the Truth, then it becomes abundantly meaningful to believe that the stability of the world that you study as a scientist reflects the stability of His upholding power, and that the truth of the generalizations and expectations that you build on the basis of scientific observation and scientific precedent is a reflection of the truthfulness, or faithfulness, of His character. Do you see the relationship here? It's not a simple one, but in a sense it's a very direct one.

QUESTION 8:
*When you say that the meaning of science is that now our responsibility is enhanced, I take it you mean we have this responsibility from a source independent of science, because science doesn't give us that responsibility. Would you agree with this?*

MACKAY:
Yes. And when I discussed responsibility I didn't, as it were, parcel it out as so much responsibility to our fellow men and so much responsibility to God. I would say it's both. But a man who doesn't find himself able to believe in God would still be able to recognize that he is answerable to his fellow men, if he is a scientist and knows the consequences of a particular act or situation. Because he is a scientist he is answerable to his fellow men to a greater extent than if he didn't have that scientific knowledge. That was really the point I was driving at.

And I would then go on to say that the man who believes in God recognizes that whatever his fellow men think about his responsibility, God will hold him answerable. I'd say that's why I'm anxious that we shouldn't drag our feet and pretend that science doesn't enhance our responsibility in the solid way it does, although I myself stressed the limitations of science and, you might say, put science in its place. I think that when scientists talk about the powers of science, they might be bragging, but more often they may be speaking with fear and trembling, because once a scientist has knowledge, he has the power that goes along with it, and he can't honestly back away from the responsibility it creates.

QUESTION 9:
*You've said that science investigates a certain order which may be suspended at certain points so that we get things we didn't expect. But this is only because there is another, larger order. Have you any suggestions about how these two orders are integrated, or do we have to live our lives with a feeling that we belong to both of them and that they are incompatible?*

MACKAY:
Well, yes. I tried to indicate the integration point partway through the lecture when I said that it is the same God whose faithfulness to His pattern of precedent justifies our day-to-day scientific expectations, Who has also expressed His faithfulness to us, His creatures, at a personal level—the level of our need for rescue from our self-centeredness, and reconciliation with our Creator. This is what the Gospel calls redemption by the death and resurrection of Christ. So I was suggesting that it's a mistake to interpret Christian doctrine to mean that a scientist should expect miracles to be happening all the time, as if God took pleasure in breaking with precedent. That is not what it implies. What it implies is that unless His personal purpose demands a break from this normal pattern, we have no biblical grounds for seeing Him as *likely* to violate our normal scientific expecta-

tions. The resurrection of Christ was a unique event for a unique *personal* purpose. But it was a purpose that expresses God's love for men, which is also expressed, according to the Bible, in the faithfulness with which He sends His rain and all the other predictable phenomena—winter and summer, cold and heat, and so forth—on which we rely. As I see it, it is God's faithfulness as Creator that integrates the two.